Tarantula Vs Bird

Mary Meinking

www.raintreepublishers.co.uk
Visit our website to find out
more information about
Raintree books.

To order:
☎ Phone 0845 6044371
📄 Fax +44 (0) 1865 312263
📠 Email myorders@raintreepublishers.co.uk

Customers from outside the UK please telephone +44 1865 312262

Raintree is an imprint of Capstone Global Library Limited,
a company incorporated in England and Wales having its
registered office at 7 Pilgrim Street, London, EC4V 6LB
– Registered company number: 6695582

Edited by Rebecca Rissman, Dan Nunn,
    and Catherine Veitch
Designed by Joanna Hinton Malivoire
Levelling by Jeanne Clidas
Picture research by Hannah Taylor
Production by Victoria Fitzgerald
Originated by Capstone Global Library
Printed and bound in China by CTPS

ISBN 978 1 406 21868 8
14 13 12 11 10
10 9 8 7 6 5 4 3 2 1

British Library Cataloguing in Publication Data
Meinking, Mary.
Tarantula vs bird. -- (Predator vs prey)
591.5'3-dc22
A full catalogue record for this book is available from the
British Library.

Acknowledgements
We would like to thank the following for permission
to reproduce photographs: p. 11 © James Degaspari
(Ecofoto.com.br); p. 14 © Sinésio Dioliveira; p. 26 ©
Sinésio Dioliveira; Alamy Images pp. 4 (© Petra Wegner),
13 (© blickwinkel), 15 (© Michael Doolittle), 17 (© Ray
Wilson), 28 (© Picture Contact); ardea.com pp. 16 (© Don
Hadden), 21 (© John S. Dunning); FLPA pp. 8 (Minden
Pictures/Claus Meyer), 19 (Minden Pictures/Claus Meyer),
23 (Minden Pictures/Thomas Marent), 29 (Minden
Pictures/Mark Moffett); Natural Visions p. 9 (Francesco
Tomasinelli); Photolibrary pp. 12 (Oxford Scientific),
18 (Morales), 25 (Oxford Scientific/John Mitchell), 27
(Oxford Scientific/Michael Fogden); Photoshot pp. 5
(NHPA/ Haroldo Palo Jr.), 10 (NHPA/ Haroldo Palo Jr.),
20 (NHPA/ Nick Garbutt), 22 (NHPA/ Haroldo Palo Jr.), 6
(NHPA/ James Carmichael Jr.), 7 (NHPA/ Haroldo Palo Jr.).

Cover photographs of a Peruvian Pinktoe Tarantula
reproduced with permission of FLPA (Minden Pictures/
Mark Moffett), and a Red-crested Finch reproduced with
permission of Photoshot (NHPA/ Haroldo Palo Jr.).

We would like to thank Michael Bright for his invaluable
help in the preparation of this book.

Every effort has been made to contact copyright holders
of material reproduced in this book. Any omissions will
be rectified in subsequent printings if notice is given to
the publisher.

Disclaimer
All the Internet addresses (URLs) given in this book were
valid at the time of going to press. However, due to the
dynamic nature of the Internet, some addresses may
have changed, or sites may have changed or ceased to
exist since publication. While the author and publisher
regret any inconvenience this may cause readers, no
responsibility for any such changes can be accepted by
either the author or the publisher.

Some words are shown in bold, **like this**. You can find
out what they mean by looking in the glossary.

Contents

Fang to feather combat

Fangs pierce! Wings beat! Two animals clash in this battle! Here's one of the creepiest creatures in the **rainforest**, the tarantula. It's up against a chirping challenger, the finch.

Pink-toed tarantula

Red-crested finch

5

The competitors live in South America. Both have strengths that'll help them in this battle.

PREDATOR
Pink-toed tarantula

LENGTH: 13 centimetres

WEIGHT: 29.5 grammes

NUMBER OF EGGS LAID AT A TIME: 50 to 200

Key

 where these types of tarantulas and finches live

Red-crested finch

LENGTH: 13.5 centimetres

WEIGHT: 11 grammes

NUMBER OF EGGS LAID AT A TIME: 2

South America

Creepy crawlers

The tarantula is covered in fur-like hairs. It uses these hairs to feel **vibrations,** or movements, nearby.

DID YOU KNOW?
Tarantulas don't have teeth. After catching **prey**, they **inject** them with juices from their fangs. That turns the prey's insides to **liquid** so the tarantula can slurp them up!

Fierce finches

The **male** finch has a red crest of feathers on its head. The finch's crest makes it look scary to an enemy.

DID YOU KNOW?
A finch may use its sharp beak to protect itself if an enemy gets too close.

Who's hungry?

The tarantula usually eats insects, lizards, or tree frogs. It will eat anything that wanders too close. After a big meal it can go for almost a week without eating.

Along came a spider

The finch flies to its nest with a big insect. Inside the nest hide two hungry babies. The pink-toed tarantula lives in a nest in the same tree. Its hairs feel the tree branch moving. It knows there must be something nearby to eat.

This tarantula has made a nest out of leaves and spider silk.

15

The chicks peck and pull the squirming insect apart. They are enjoying their meal. The parent finch flies off to search for more food for its young.

DID YOU KNOW?

Tarantulas have eight eyes! But they can't see very well. They need their hairs to show them the way to their next meal.

17

The tarantula moves very slowly towards its **prey**. It climbs up the tree. Its hair-covered body helps it move quietly. The young finches finish off the insect. They wait for their parents to bring them more food.

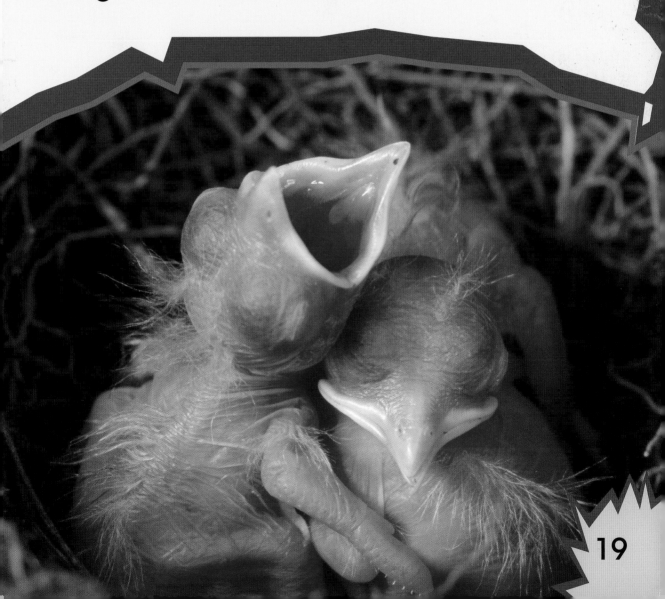

The tarantula quietly sneaks down the branch towards the nest. When the tarantula is close, it **charges** at the nest. The baby birds are too young to fly away and escape. The **male** finch swoops to the rescue. It squawks out a warning call.

The finch hovers over the nest. It pecks the tarantula with its beak. The **female** finch hears the squawking and shoots towards the nest. She also starts pecking the tarantula.

DID YOU KNOW?

When a tarantula is **threatened**, it tries to look bigger and meaner. It lifts its front legs off the ground and shows its fangs.

23

The tarantula rears up! But it doesn't scare the birds. The **male** finch slams into the tarantula and knocks it off the branch. The tarantula falls out of the tree. It spreads its legs out and floats through the air. It lands softly on the forest floor below.

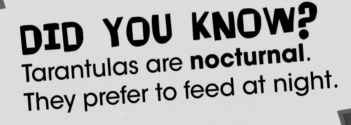

DID YOU KNOW?
Tarantulas are **nocturnal**. They prefer to feed at night.

DID YOU KNOW?
A tarantula has a claw on each leg. It can draw each claw in, just like a cat!

And the winner is...

...the finch! When finches work together, they can chase away almost any **predator**. Living in the trees of the **rainforest** helps too. Not many predators will climb all the way up the tree to their nests. So their young are safe for now.

What are the Odds?

The pink-toed tarantula doesn't usually eat birds. Sometimes the giant spider will find baby birds alone and eat them. But usually the parents are close by and won't let that happen. So the pink-toed tarantula has to wait for other **prey** to hop, buzz, or slither by.

tree frog

Glossary

charge rush or attack

female members of a species that give birth to young

inject force a liquid into something

liquid fluid, such as water

male members of a species that don't give birth

nocturnal at night-time

predator animal that hunts other animals

prey animal that is hunted by other animals for food

rainforest thick, warm-weather forest that has heavy rainfall

threatened made to feel in danger

vibration shaking movement

Find out more

Books

Hiding in Rainforests, Deborah Underwood
(Raintree Publishers, 2010)

Rainforests, Lucy Beckett-Bowman
(Usborne Publishers, 2008)

Tarantula, Anita Ganeri (Raintree Publishers, 2010)

Websites

**http://kids.nationalgeographic.com/Animals/
CreatureFeature/Tarantulas**
Visit this website to learn about tarantulas and
watch videos of them in the rainforest.

http://ran.org/rainforestheroes/
This website has lots of information about
rainforests, the animals that live there, and how we
need to protect them.

**http://www.rainforest-alliance.org/education.
cfm?id=kidsmain**
Explore this website to find out more about
rainforest animals and enjoy the activities.

Index